WELSH WALKS AND LEGENDS
Showell Styles

Book designed with the support of the Welsh Arts Council.

Lay-out, photographs and drawings by Elwyn Davies.
Cover design and type-setting by Design Systems Limited, Cardiff.
Cover photographs by courtesy of Wales Tourist Board.
Printed and bound by CSP Ltd., Cardiff.

SBN 902375 19 9 Paperbound
    902375 20 2 Casebound

JOHN JONES CARDIFF LTD

CONTENTS

To Mums and Dads who still like to use their legs.

INTRODUCTION

orth Wales is a land of legends. Some of them are fairy-tales, some are love-stories, and others are history — or something like it. Many of them are attached to places, in the hills or on the sea-coast; others centre on an old building or even a rock, to which local people will point and say 'It must have happened, because that is still there to prove it!'

This book tells some of the legends, and helps you to see for yourself just where these strange, or comic, or dramatic happenings of long ago took place. Short and easy walks from where you leave the car are usually involved, with one or two longer ones included for the energetic. You won't need mountaineering clothes or climbing-boots and none of these legend-walks will take more than half-a-day unless you care to spin it out by taking a picnic along.

The stories come from six popular tourist districts of North Wales and are grouped under district headings, but if you have a car all the walks described can be done from any one of the centres named.

I shall tell the story of the legend first, then describe how to get to its location. The Map Square numbers will enable you to spot on the Sketch Map what part of North Wales you are bound for. Ordnance Survey map Grid References are also given for those who like map-reading; Sheet 107 (Snowdon) covers all the walks except three on Sheet 108, one on Sheet 115, and one on Sheet 116.

I did all the walks myself in the autumn of 1971 and the spring of 1972, and at that time the paths and routes described were open and public, with no access impediments. There is unlikely to be any change; but if there is, I must disclaim responsibility for any trouble that may arise. As to the legends: often there are several different versions of the story, and in these cases I've simply picked the one I liked best.

VALE OF LLANGOLLEN

Nest and her lovers

The white hart of Llangar

Myfanwy of Dinas Bran

NEST AND HER LOVERS

ing Henry the First of England was no more restrained in his passions than any other powerful ruler of the twelfth century. It made little difference to him that the beautiful Nest, daughter of the Welsh prince Rhys ap Tudor, had been placed in his care as a Royal Ward; he fell in love with Nest and seduced her, and she bore him a son.

In those days, however, there was an accepted way of dealing with such a situation. Nest's baby son was named Duke of Gloucester, and King Henry gave Nest in marriage to one of his barons, Gerald de Windsor — who, it seems, was in love with her himself. Gerald was Earl of Pembroke, and took his new wife with him to South Wales, where the fame of her beauty soon spread far beyond those parts — as far, even, as the kingdoms of Gwynedd and Powys in the north. Though Gerald was a Norman baron and maintained an armed force in Pembroke Castle, he was on terms of slightly uneasy peace with Prince Cadwgan, Welsh ruler of this land of Ceredigion as well as of Powys, and the Earl and Countess lived in peace and happiness for a year. Then came a Christmas when Cadwgan ordained a great Eisteddfod in South Wales, to which everyone of distinction flocked, including the Welsh countess. And with the guests came Cadwgan's daredevil son Owain.

Now Owain lived in his father's second kingdom of Powys, in a hunting-lodge called Plas Eglwyseg at the head of a secret glen north of the Dee. Here he had gathered about him a band of reckless fighting-men, with whom he would sally forth by the path he called his war path to hunt, or raid, or harass King Henry's men-at-arms. He was accustomed to take for himself whatever he wanted. And when he came to his father's Eisteddfod and set eyes on the lovely Nest he determined at once to carry her off. That very night he and his men broke into the castle of Pembroke, set it on fire, and dragged Nest from the bed where she was sleeping with her husband. The Earl, naked and unarmed, escaped with his life by way of a drainpipe. Nest was borne away across the mountains to Owain's retreat at Plas Eglwyseg, where (it appears) she lived quite happily with her captor for some time.

But the mad action of Owain ap Cadwgan brought terrible consequences. King Henry, appealed to by Gerald de Windsor, ordered Prince Cadwgan to restore the stolen countess on pain of losing his kingdoms. Cadwgan's attempts to comply met with flat defiance from his son, who eluded all efforts to capture him; and war broke out through the whole of Wales. Norman barons aided Cadwgan's Welsh rivals to take Powys from him and others robbed him of much of his southern kingdom. The new rulers of Powys disinherited Owain and at last succeeded in driving him out of his refuge at Plas Eglwyseg, whence he fled to Ireland, leaving Nest homeless. The deserted beauty made her way southward and after a long and hazardous journey reached Pembroke Castle, where Earl Gerald — now the most powerful lord in South Wales — took her in his arms and once more established her as his wife and countess.

And now, for a year or more, there was a period of peace. It was broken by the arrival of a raiding force from Ireland, which was opposed by the Earl of Pembroke in alliance with the Welsh. Owain had accompanied the raiders, but now elected to change sides and fight for his native land. In the midst of the battle Gerald recognised the man who had wronged him fighting on the same side as himself. Changing the direction of his attack, he and his bodyguard fell upon Owain and slew him, thus wiping out, to the satisfaction of everyone who counted in those days, the dishonour he had suffered at Owain's hands.

Gerald de Windsor ended his warlike career by dying peacefully in his castle of Carew, but his wife's career was not finished thereby. Though her children were now grown up and married, Nest still had her beauty — and plenty of love to spare. She transferred her affections first to Stephen, Constable of Caernarfon Castle, and then to the Sheriff of Pembroke, presenting each of them with a son. All her children, legitimate or illegitimate, founded great families; and if you are a Fitzgerald, a Carew, a Barry, or a Fitzstephen you are very probably of 'the race of Nesta.'

THE WALK :
TO PLAS EGLWYSEG
AND WORLD'S END

MAP SQUARE D2
O.S. reference 229479
Suitable for the Under Eights,
being a short walk at the end
of a car ride.

Out of the holiday season it's a quiet 10-mile walk from Llangollen to World's End and back, but in summer there are likely to be a fair number of cars making the trip and the lanes are narrow. Take the car, then, and start from Llangollen.

If arriving by the A5, turn through the town and cross the bridge over the Dee. On the far side turn right for a few yards only, then left, uphill, crossing the Llangollen canal by a bridge and turning left again, with the School (Ysgol Dinas Bran) on your right. The lane you are on mounts gently for ¼-mile, then you bear right − signpost WORLD'S END 4. From here onward the lane is narrow and winding, with occasional passing-places. The limestone escarpment called Eglwyseg Rocks is sighted, and soon you are driving along the foot of it and entering a steep-sided glen. The lane becomes narrower still, requiring slow and careful driving. When a specta-cular limestone precipice is seen towering above the glen in front, you are close to the site of the hunting-lodge to which Owain ap Cadwgan carried off the lovely Nest.

On today's Ordnance Survey maps the place is named 'Plas Uchaf,' the Upper Hall. An Elizabethan manor house, black-and-white half-timbered, stands on the foundations of the old hall, with a large inscription across the front: LX III

ELIZABETH REGINA. According to the present owner Queen Elizabeth 1 once stayed here, reputedly to have a baby. He also asserts that Winston Churchill and General Goering stayed here on a shooting holiday in 1936/37. It's not easy to say whether these tales are more, or less, historical than the story of Owain and Nest!

A few yards uphill beyond the house is an iron gate. The lane goes on uphill beyond the gate, climbing a more open section of the glen, and the car can be turned and parked here close to the stream that comes down below a forested slope. The limestone crag already mentioned rises splendidly overhead; its name is Craig-y-Cythraul — the Devil's Crag.

For a short walk (20 minutes to half-an-hour) walk on up the hill for 5 minutes, to where the lane turns sharp left and goes through a ford. There is a stile on the right leading into the forest. You may be surprised at the signpost beside it, a carved oaken board with the words LLWYBYR CLAWDD OFFA. Llwybyr is the Welsh word for a footpath, and clawdd means 'dyke.' By crossing the stile you can go a little way along the ancient line of Offa's Dyke, that extraordinary boundary of bank-and-ditch built by the King of Mercia four centuries before Owain's love-affair with Nest.

The path through the forestry trees is pleasant and easy to follow. In a few hundred yards you come to a stile crossing a fence, where an older and sparser wood begins. Go over the stile and turn steeply downhill beside the fence. At the bottom a log footbridge takes you across the stream and so back to where you left the car.

THE WHITE HART OF LLANGAR

ong ago in the peaceful valley of the Afon Dyfrdwy, which Saxons call the River Dee, the pious dwellers in the district of Edeirnion resolved to build a church. It would not be very big (for at that time there were not many people in those parts) but it would be the Church of All Saints, they decided, and built in a place where the Christian folk of the valley could all get to it on Sundays.

Three greyheaded elders took charge of the work and many younger men helped in the carrying of stones and the clearing of the ground. They had chosen a place where the paths from several villages met, a level site that had building materials in plenty ready to hand, and by mustering every man capable of work and starting at dawn of a summer day they made amazing progress. The first course of huge stones was already in place when darkness fell.

Next morning the builders met again on the site, eager to raise the church walls two or three courses higher. To their utter astonishment there was no sign of the work they had so well begun the day before. The pile of raw material was still there, but all the stones they had placed in position with so much labour had vanished. It would have needed an army of men to carry the great stones away, so the builders knew that some kind of supernatural agency was at work. After a grave discussion, the three elders gave the word to start building the church again. The workers succeeded in regaining all the ground they had lost by this mysterious interference, and went home at nightfall weary but well-content.

On the second morning there was again no sign of their day's work. Every stone had vanished. And again, stubbornly refusing to be frightened or discouraged, they rebuilt the first course of the church walls. On the third morning things were exactly the same — all their work was undone. But this time the three greybeards, after an excited conference, told the church-builders to go to their homes and await word from them. For the elders had discovered that in the night each of them had received the same vision — a bright light shining from above, and a voice saying 'Seek the white hart, and where you see him, there build your church.' None of the three doubted that only by following this command would they succeed in getting their church finished, and with one accord they set off in different directions to look for the hart, or stag, of this unusual colour.

All that day they wandered, searching, through the woods and thickets that clothed the Berwyn slopes along the valley of the Dyfrdwy river; all that day until darkness was falling, with many a glimpse of the tawny-hued deer but never one of a white hart. They had arranged to meet at a place in the river valley near where the Alwen stream flows into the Dyfrdwy, and here at dusk the three came together, tired and despairing. With little spoken, they were about to make their way to their homes when, suddenly, they all saw a great White Hart standing on the hillside a little way above the river bank. For an instant he stood, seeming to look down at them; then he vanished, never to reappear.

Next morning, at the summons of the elders, the workmen began to carry the building materials to the place where the hart had stood. When they began to build, the work seemed twice as easy as before and was never interfered with. The walls rose with remarkable speed, the roof seemed almost to grow from the walls, and soon the church was finished.

It was duly sanctified as the Church of All Saints. But to all the people of Edeirnion it was known as Llan-Garw-Gwyn — garw meaning 'stag' and gwyn meaning 'white.' In after years the name was shortened, becoming first Llangarw and then Llangar. And to this day the old church, standing in its curious place remote from villages and with no road to it, is called Llangar.

THE WALK :
TO LLANGAR CHURCH

MAP SQUARE D3
O.S. reference 063424
Short and easy walk; ½-hour,
could be extended to an hour.

This walk is based on Corwen, and could be done on foot from a car parked at the disused railway station. However, this would involve ¾-mile along a fairly busy road and it's probably more reasonable to do the road part by car.

If you come into Corwen from the Llangollen direction, bear left off the A5 before crossing the river bridge at the end of the town. If you come from the Betws-y-coed direction, cross this bridge; don't enter the town, but at once turn sharp right, uphill, on B4401.

In about half-a-mile this road curves to the right across a stone bridge. Beyond the bridge it has wide grass verges, and when these show themselves look out for a lane on the right — the first you come to. The car can be parked on the verge.

Walk down the lane, towards the river, passing a farm on the left. 50 yards past the farm turn right, across a brook and through an iron gate. The rough way beyond is the old approach to the church and soon ends at an ancient lych-gate. The church is tiny, and is now disused. Its churchyard is a chaos of extremely aged tombstones, some of which have stone rests near them for the comfort of those offering prayers for the dead. The tall yewtrees that overshadow it must also be an immense age.

[Note : In November 1972 the church was entirely encased in corrugated iron, pending repairs, and looked like a large barn. No one could tell me how soon the repairs would be complete.]

If someone is willing to take the car back to Corwen, or if you have got this far on foot, you could return as follows : go back through the iron gate and gain the disused railway track by a stile; turn right, and with slightly rough walking — the river close on your left — you can reach the ruinous station at Corwen in 25 minutes.

MYFANWY OF DINAS BRÂN

he old story-spinners told of a hero named Brân who built a dinas, or city, on the great mound above the Dyfrdwy vale; and that was as long ago as the Bronze Age. The centuries rolled by, and there came one of the Lords of Ial (a forerunner of the Yale who founded the great American college) to make a more habitable fortress on the ditches and parapets of the old dinas. But about the year 1250 a stone castle began to rise on the great mound, every stone of its walls carried to the summit by gangs of serfs or prisoners. Castell Dinas Brân was the work of the Norman barons who were determined to subdue the rebellious Welsh.

But there were treaties and agreements — even inter-marrying — between the great Welsh families and the Norman nobles. And a hundred years after the building of Castell Dinas Brân the fortress was held by a Vychan of the house of Tudor Trevor, whose overlord was the Norman Earl of Arundel and whose daughter Myfanwy was the most beautiful maiden in all the land of Powys.

Myfanwy was well aware of her beauty. But like many a pretty girl before and since, she liked nothing better than to hear her beauty praised. Many men, young and handsome, warriors and of good birth, thronged the hall of Castell Dinas Brân to seek her favour. Myfanwy Vychan spurned them all, for they lacked the thing she most desired — the gift of weaving poetry and music that reflected as in a mirror her wondrous beauty. The one man who possessed this gift was a youthful bard, penniless and of lowly birth, who dwelt in the valley below the castle. His name was Hywel ap Einion.

Hywel had fallen madly in love with Myfanwy, and every day he toiled up the long, steep ascent to the castle with his harp, hoping to be admitted to the hall where he could play and sing to Myfanwy Vychan. Sometimes he would be allowed to enter, sometimes he was sent away. But whenever he was admitted to Myfanwy's presence he played and sang to her so wonderfully — always praising her unrivalled beauty in a flood of wild words and enchanting music — that she would neither listen to nor look at any man of those around her, but Hywel ap Einion. And the young bard came to believe that she returned his love.

Too soon his hope was shattered. A suitor more handsome, more powerful, and (perhaps) more articulate than the others came wooing. The match was a suitable one for the heiress of the Tudor Trevors and in the ensuing betrothal festivities the poor bard was quite forgotten. There was not a word for him, nor even a look, from the beauty of Castell Dinas Brân by way of farewell.

Hywel climbed no more to the castle on the hilltop. Broken-hearted, he wandered through the Dyfrdwy forests with his harp; and as he went he composed the Ode which was to live for more than four hundred years as one of the best-loved Welsh poems. It was a very long Ode, and of its many lines four can be translated into English thus :

> 'Far from Myfanwy's marble towers
> I pass my solitary hours.
> O thou that shinest like the sky,
> Behold thy faithful Hywel die!'

But Hywel did not die of his broken heart. And as for the cruel Myfanwy Vychan, to whom he sang —

> 'Fairer thou and colder too,
> Than winter snow on Aran's brow' —

her undeserved reward was to be made famous by her humble lover's poem. So that to this day, when Castell Dinas Brân is a lifeless ruin, her story lives on.

THE WALK :
TO CASTELL DINAS BRÂN

MAP SQUARE D2
O.S. reference 223431
Steep paths, fine views. Allow
1½ hours up and down.

Start on foot from the public car park in Llangollen. (To drive to this car park, turn off the A5 at the traffic lights halfway through the town, and take the first street on the left.) From the car park make for the bridge across the Dee, cross it, and turn right. Almost at once turn left up Wharf Hill, a lesser road that ascends over the canal bridge. Opposite the bridge you'll see a signpost showing the start of the path to Castell Dinas Brân.

First the path mounts past the school (called Ysgol Dinas Brân) and then becomes a lane for a short time. Beyond a second signpost it climbs to an open hill-ridge with the ruined castle above on the right. Parents should keep a wary eye on younger children from now on; the hillsides are scarcely precipices, but there are steep places below the ruined wall where a tumble could have nasty results.

There's not a great deal left of the old castle, and it's anyone's guess where the castle hall used to be that saw Hywel ap Einion's musical courtship of cruel Myfanwy Vychan. The chief charm of the place is its magnificent situation and views. From this height of 1,060 feet above the sea you can see eastward into England as far as the Wrekin and westward to Snowdon — but for Snowdon you'll need an exceptionally clear day.

The quickest way down is the way you came up. But a pleasant alternative that takes about 10 minutes longer is to go down on the opposite side. Keep the distant Dee and its companion the Llangollen canal on your right front as you start down from the castle, and you'll quickly see a stile over the fence below. Cross this, keep on steeply down for a couple of minutes, and you reach a stile that gives access to a lane. Turn right on the lane, which has delightful views on the left as you curl rightward round the hill and descend to a house entrance. Opposite this entrance a Public Footpath sign guides you across fields on the right — keep quite level for the first 5 minutes — and this brings you back into your route of ascent at the second 'Dinas Bran' signpost. Turn left here, and you can be back at the car in 20 minutes.

CONWAY VALLEY
The legend of the Afanc
The stone women of Moelfre
Taliesin the bard

THE LEGEND OF THE AFANC

ong ago, before histories began to be written, the people of the Vale of Conway were sorely troubled by a monster who lived in a pool of the river. This afanc, as he was called, was an enormous beast that possessed supernatural powers, which he used (when he was in a vicious mood) to cause disastrous floods, ruining the crops and drowning the cattle. Spear and dart and sword had been tried against him by the bravest of the young men, but no weapon forged by man could make any impression on the afanc's scaly hide. The greybeards held conference, and decided that there was only one thing to do : the monster must be got out of his pool and taken far away to some other lake beyond the mountains.

Preparations began at once. Strong iron chains were forged, and the two mightiest oxen in the land — the giant long-horned animals belonging to Hu Gadarn — were brought to Betws-y-coed, for the afanc pool was close to this place. But the problem of how to get the afanc out of the pool, so that he could be chained to the oxen, had still be to solved. Now the monster was known to be very partial to beautiful maidens, showing in this at least one human quality; and when this was remembered, a courageous damsel was found who agreed to act as decoy. The lake to which the afanc was to be dragged was chosen — Llyn Ffynnon Las, under the peak of Snowdon — and all was ready.

The giant oxen and the men with the chains hid themselves in the woods near the pool while the damsel sat by the water's edge and called softly to the afanc. By-and-by the hideous monster came wallowing up out of the depths, and — yielding to the girl's enticements — heaved himself ashore and laid his ugly head in her lap. Now, or never, was the moment! The men leaped from their concealment and deftly wound the chains round the afanc, who saw too late the trick that had been played upon him. Furious, he struck at the girl with his great claws, tearing her breast, and hurled himself back into the pool.

But the chains were already harnessed to the oxen, and slowly, with every man present lending his strength to help, the afanc was drawn out. All up the rocky Lledr valley they dragged him, as far as the spot where Dolwyddelan stands now; and striking north-west over the shoulder of Moel Siabod they crossed the watershed and came into the head of the Gwynant valley. So great were the efforts of the oxen that the eye of one of them dropped out, causing it to shed floods of tears which formed the pool called ever afterwards Pwll Llygad yr Ych, the Pool of the Ox's Eye.

The last part of the oxen's labour was the hardest. They dragged the afanc up into Cwm Dyli, past Llyn Llydaw, and at last reached the lake, 1,970 feet above sea-level, which is now called Glaslyn but whose proper name is Llyn Ffynnon Las, the Lake of the Blue Fountain. On the shores of the lake, with Snowdon summit frowning overhead, the men loosed the chains. The monster plunged headlong into Glaslyn at once, and sank from sight in the immensely deep blue water. And there, the old folk in Beddgelert village will tell you, he dwells to this day.

THE WALK :
TO THE AFANC POOL

MAP SQUARE C2
O.S. reference 798546
Easy and short (¾-mile) but can
be extended to the Fairy Glen.

The walk starts in Betws-y-coed. Though the car could in fact be taken right to the Afanc Pool (called the Beaver Pool in some guidebooks) it's a pleasant walk on a minor road, through trees and beside the river for much of the way. If you're staying in Betws you'll want to walk anyway; if you drive in, park in the car park by Betws-y-coed station. There is a restaurant here, by the way.

When you come out of the station drive, turn left along the main road for about 200 yards. Just before the road crosses the railway, a minor road turns uphill to the right. Follow this. It quickly leaves the houses behind and becomes a leafy lane. You pass under a railway bridge that carries the single-track line to Blaenau Ffestiniog (one of the most beautiful rail trips in Britain) and soon afterwards the lane is running along the bank of the River Conway. There is more than one fine pool, but the Afanc Pool is the big one near the junction of the lane with a bigger road, A496, which crosses the river by a stone bridge just here, ¾-mile from the start of the lane.

The Afanc Pool is large and deep and rather gloomy under its big trees. No description of an afanc has been left by the people who claimed to have seen one, but no doubt he was a horrific monster, and on any but the brighter days the pool looks a suitable home for him. A little scrambly path leads down to its shore, and as there is no afanc there now it's quite safe to go down and do a bit of minor exploration.

This walk has occupied about half-an-hour so far. It's well worth extending it to see the Fairy Glen.

The entrance to this deservedly famous beauty-spot is only a couple of minutes' walk from the Afanc Pool. Go to the junction with A496, turn left across the bridge, and turn right up a signposted lane immediately beyond the bridge. The lane brings you to the Fairy Glen in any easy 15 minutes' walking, and the way can't be missed.

For those who like exploration, there is another little route that should be mentioned. Having crossed the bridge and taken the Fairy Glen lane, look for a narrow gap in the right-hand wall just 50 yards up the lane. If you go through the gap, a steep little path takes you down to the river bank. Turn left here, and you will come to some waterworn rock scenery by the big pool where the Lledr joins the Conway; or turn right, and in a few yards you can scramble under the arch of the road bridge to a fine rock seat out on the other side, overlooking the Afanc Pool.

THE STONE WOMEN OF MOELFRE

n the fields by the shores of Conway Bay the corn had been harvested. The oxen had trodden the grain from the ears, and the chaff and the grain lay together waiting to be winnowed. The winnowing was done by the women, who would have to work for hour after hour, tossing up the chaff and grain into the wind so that the lighter chaff would be blown away and the heavier grain left ready for the miller. But for days there had not been a breath of wind in the fields by the sea. Only on the tall hills that curved round to the headland of Penmaenmawr was there any wind.

The women grew impatient. The rain might come, soaking grain and chaff together, and rob them of the good flour from which they made their bread.

'There's plenty of wind up on Moelfre,' said one woman, who wore a red kirtle. 'Let's carry the corn in sacks and winnow it up there.'

She said this on a Sunday. And in Wales no man, woman, or child was ever to be seen working on a Sunday.

'We would be breaking the Sabbath,' said another, whose kirtle was white.

'What then?' retorted her neighbour. 'Doesn't the wind blow on a Sunday, and shall we waste it and lose the good flour?'

'That's sense,' nodded a third woman, in a blue kirtle. 'I'll get three sacks and we three will carry the corn up to Moelfre.'

So the three women filled the sacks and started up the hillside, bent beneath their loads. They passed a cottage, and here an old man called loudly after them, warning them that they sinned in breaking the Sabbath and would be punished. Higher up they passed a farm, and here the farmer came out to give them the same solemn warning. The three laden women laughed at the warnings and toiled on.

They climbed the steep glen where once men had used the hard Graig Lwyd stone to make primitive axes. They gained the lofty crest where the Meini Hirion — the

27

Long Stones — stood in a wide circle. There was still no wind, but the round summit called Moelfre was not far away and they knew there would be wind up there. They carried their sacks to the very top of the hill, emptied them in a heap, and began the winnowing, throwing up the corn into the steady breeze that was blowing there.

And then came the dreadful happening which Sir John Wynn recorded in his book published in the seventeenth century. 'These faythles women, regardynge there profytt more than the obsearvynge of God's commandements,' were instantly turned into three stones, one red, one white, and one blue.

There are no coloured stones on the top of Moelfre now. But a little searching will reveal, sunk in the turf of the summit, the tops of three grey rocks; as if the Stone Women of Moelfre had at last been permitted to sink into the very ground.

THE WALK :
TO MOELFRE AND
THE DRUIDS' CIRCLE

MAP SQUARE B1
O.S. reference 716745
The longest walk in this book, including a climb to 1,423 feet. 4 hours up and down. Leave the Under Eights behind.

The start is in Penmaenmawr, 3½ miles west of Conway on A55. The free car park is near the centre of the town, just off A55; on your left if you come from the Conway direction, on your right if you come from Bangor. Park here. At the car park exit turn sharp right and follow the uphill road called Y Berllan, which curves right and then left, ending at the upper limit of houses where there is a fork of two narrow lanes. Take the left-hand (stony) lane.

This lane or bridle-path mounts gently into a green valley under steep hillsides.

High on your right are the Graig Lwyd quarries, working noisily if it is a weekday. In 5 minutes or so the bridle-path comes to a wider road crossing it — Craig Lwyd Road. Turn to the right up this road. In 200 yards you come to a farmhouse on the left, with a gate leading to a footpath (signposted) going up on the left of the house.

The footpath climbs along the side of the green valley, zigzagging when it gets steep. Down on the left are the mounds and scars where, archaeologists say, primitive man extracted the stone for the 'Graig Lwyd' axes; stone axes that undoubtedly came from Penmaenmawr have been found all over Britain. Up in the head of the valley the path goes to the left, crossing a boggy patch by a concrete causeway and just afterwards passing through a wall by a gap with a signpost above it. Go up beside the wall, and join a broader pathway a few yards higher, turning to the right along it. In two or three minutes you will reach a level space on the crest of the hills, with a domed hill standing above. The hill is Moelfre, and an easy climb of about 200 feet brings you to the summit and a very fine view. The height here is 1,423 feet above the sea, which stretches to the far horizon on the north. Anglesey is in sight to westward, and east and south are mountains.

The non-appearance of the Stone Women may be disappointing, but the Meini Hirion will make up for it. The so-called Druids' Circle (the stones were placed here long before the Druids) is one of the finest of its kind in Wales, and is only about ten minutes' walk from Moelfre. Descend from the hill and follow the grassy path that runs level — or nearly so — along the crest, with the sea down on your left. Soon you will come to a circle of rocks, close on the right of the path; these are also primitive remains, but the Meini Hirion themselves are a short distance farther. The circle, of quite large rocks, may be as much as 4,000 years old, and was probably an early form of observatory. However, it was undoubtedly used as a place of sacrifice in the early Bronze Age, for investigators discovered, in an urn at the centre of the circle, the

29

cremated remains of a child, together with a bronze knife.

There are several ways of extending this walk. By turning back from Meini Hirion, for instance, and following the path westward, you would come down into Llanfair-fechan by way of Nant-y-pandy. Rather than walk along the coast road for 2½ miles, though, most people will prefer to go down by the way they came up: return to the wall below Moelfre, go through the signposted gap, and down to the Craig Lwyd road and so to the car park.

TALIESIN THE BARD

lphin, son of Gwyddno Garanhir, was the unluckiest prince in all the history of Wales. His father, who ruled over Mid Wales in the sixth century, gave him a large province as his estate; and almost immediately the sea broke the defensive dams of that estate and it was lost beneath the waves. By way of comforting him, Gwyddno presented this unfortunate young man with the annual salmon-netting of the Dovey river, which was the equivalent of giving him a large present of money, so vast was the number of salmon usually caught. But Elphin's bad luck stayed with him. As he watched the river-keeper and his servants working the nets, he saw that there was not a single fish in them. Indeed, the only object to emerge from the river was a large leather bag that had lodged on the edge of the weir. It was a thousand chances to one that there was nothing of worth in the leather bag, but Elphin bade the river-keeper bring it to him. This was done and the bag was opened. Inside was a small boy, hardly more than a babe but very much alive.

'Tal-iesin!' exclaimed the river-keeper; which means 'How radiant is his brow!' : for the child's forehead seemed to shine with a strange lustre.

'Taliesin let him be called,' said Elphin, and set the boy on his horse and rode homeward with him, sadly at first but soon in wonder and amazement.

As they rode, the child began to speak, holding forth in an impassioned ode. This miraculous poetry told Elphin that the boy had been sent to guide him; that he was to be not only a great poet but also a great prophet, and before him all Elphin's enemies should fall.

The years passed, and from that time Elphin prospered in all he did. As for Taliesin, he became the most famous bard of Britain. Among his prophecies was that which foretold the end of the wicked king Maelgwn Gwynedd, but his most inspired odes were those that urged on the warriors of Britain in their struggle against the Saxon invaders.

Many places in Wales became associated with the name of Taliesin, especially the beautiful lake called Geirionydd, on the forested heights above the Conway valley. Here in his later years the bard used to come to meditate and seek inspiration.

To this day the sayings of this first and greatest of bards are remembered in Wales, and none more so than the famous prophecy he made, towards the end of his life, about the British of that time and their fate :

> Their Lord they shall praise,
> Their language they shall keep,
> Their land they shall lose —
> Except wild Wales.

THE WALK :
TO TALIESIN'S MONUMENT
BY LAKE GEIRIONYDD

MAP SQUARE B2
O.S. reference 765616
Steep forestry roads, mountain lake. About 4 hours excluding halts.

This is longer than most of the Legend-walks and makes a good picnic excursion. It's easy to combine it with a visit to Gwydir Castle (Elizabethan, famous for its peacocks) or with Legend-walk No. 4, the Legend of the Afanc.

From Llanrwst on A496 — 4 miles from Betws-y-coed — cross the bridge over the Conway river and so gain the crossroads on the opposite side of the valley, where B5106 is joined. This point can be reached from Conway by following B5106 southward through Dolgarrog. Gwydir Castle is 150 yards from the crossroads in the direction of Betws-y-coed. For the walk, you cross B5106 and drive up a minor road signposted *LLYN GEIRIONYDD 2½m.*, which ascends into the steep forests. Follow this road for ¼-mile only. When you reach a large red-lettered notice — *FOREST FIRE DANGER AREA* — park on the roadside near it, or turn the car and park 50 yards back down the hill, opposite a narrow lane signposted *LLYN GEIRIONYDD 2¼m.* This lane starts the walk.

(N.B. the whole walking-route is motorable — just — but in general the lanes are very narrow and very steep, and walking is a less anxious business.)

The lane is easy walking at first, then climbs steeply up into the forest. 20 minutes of this, and the angle eases as you emerge into an upper land of fields and streams. Here is the tiny hamlet called Tai, where a signpost directs you: *LLYN GEIRIONYDD 1¼.* In 10 minutes a right turn, also signposted, brings you past a farm and downhill to the lake. This last bit is delightful walking — mountains in the distance, the Crafnant glen far down on the right, and Geirionydd lake coming slowly into view on the left.

The lake beneath its fine crags and forests looks more Tyrolean or Bavarian than Welsh. At the nearer end is seen the tall stone monument to Taliesin, erected here on the place where the bard is said to have lived for a time. You reach the monument in five minutes from the road, crossing a stile on the right. There's no inscription to tell you what it is, and on some old maps it's marked *Bedd Taliesin* — Taliesin's Grave, though traditionally the bard was buried above the Dovey estuary where Elphin found the child genius.

Along the lake shore now, with lots of good picnic places halfway and an 'official' forestry picnic site with tables and benches at the south end. Here turn left opposite the farmhouse (Tal-y-llyn). This lane climbs uphill, past some old lead mines, with fine backward views. At the top of the longish ascent there's a glimpse of *Moel Siabod* on the right, and then for the next 15 minutes you walk between forestry plantations with very little up or down. Now you reach a T-junction of lanes and turn left (signpost LLANRWST) for a last bit of uphill past another old lead mine. At the top of this you're at your highest point of the walk and it's worth climbing the heathery bank on the right to look at the views. In ½-hour from here you'll be back in the car.

Downhill now, curving left past a small lake, a large lead-mine chimney, and a chapel. Then more steeply down, 1¼ miles, to your parking-place.

THE NORTH COAST
The end of Maelgwn Gwynedd
Deganwy and its castle
How Prince Madoc discovered America

f all the princes who have ruled over Gwynedd, as North Wales was once called, the most wicked was Maelgwn. Maelgwn was Prince of Gwynedd thirteen centuries ago, and this is his story.

In those days there were four petty kingdoms in Wales, and the four rulers wished to decide which of them should be Brenhin Pennaf, or chief king. It was agreed that they should meet on the sands of the Dovey estuary, bringing their thrones with them; that the thrones should be placed in a row fronting the incoming tide, with their royal owners sitting on them; and that whichever of the four stayed longest on his throne when the sea came racing in to submerge them should be declared Brenhin Pennaf.

Now Maelgwn had a cunning counsellor, Maeldav the Elder, who was determined that his master should triumph. 'Maeldav,' says the old chronicle, 'secretly prepared a throne made of wings' — and we can take it as pretty certain that these were inflated skins, to act as water-wings. At any rate, the spring tide came roaring and foaming in, and the sea rose higher and higher, until the princes from Powys and South Wales took fright and splashed their way to safety. But Maelgwn rode the waves on his floating throne, and so became chief ruler of Wales.

It was an age when men were accustomed to harsh treatment from their overlords, but Maelgwn Gwynedd overstepped all bounds of cruelty. The people of his own land cursed him for the blackness of his deeds, but there was no one strong enough to oppose him and it seemed as if the sufferings of his many victims would never be avenged. He built himself a palace close to the north coast, within bowshot of a hill-fort that had been the stronghold of his ancestors hundreds of years earlier, and here at Llys Rhos (as it was called) Maelgwn lived a life of drunkenness and excess, with other evil-doing too horrible to be told.

At last the great bard and prophet Taliesin foretold an end to the suffering of

Gwynedd. This was his prophecy: 'A wondrous beast shall come up from Morfa Rhianedd, the Sea marsh of the Maidens, to avenge the iniquities of Maelgwn. Its hair and its teeth and its eyes shall all be yellow, and this beast shall be the end of Maelgwn Gwynedd!'

The prophecy of Taliesin was fulfilled in the year 547. In that year the deadly plague which some called the Yellow Death was ravaging Europe, and spread northward into Britain. As the plague's trail of death approached the land of Gwynedd, Maelgwn's terror of it grew until he was almost mad with fear. He shut himself in his palace of Llys Rhos with a few favourite courtiers and forbade anyone to pass in or out, and for a little while it seemed that he had escaped the fate that was overtaking so many of his subjects in the world outside. But one day, hearing his name loudly called from the outer gateway, Maelgwn looked through the keyhole of the great door. A moment later he fell to the ground, writhing in agony; and his only words before he died were 'The Yellow Beast!'

The terrified courtiers fled, leaving their dead prince in the palace. And it was long indeed before anyone would venture in to bring out the body of the Brenhin Pennaf for burial; which gave rise to a saying that is remembered to this day: Hir hun y Faelgwn yn Llys Rhos – 'the long sleep of Maelgwn in the palace of Rhos.'

Llys Rhos fell into ruin. But from its stones a new palace named Llys Euryn was built, on the very spot where Maelgwn Gwynedd wrought – and paid for – his evil deeds.

THE WALK :
TO LLYS EURYN AND BRYN EURYN

MAP SQUARE C1
O.S. reference 833803
Easy. 1 hour, if halts are short.

Whether you are staying in Rhos-on-Sea or coming from Llandudno or Colwyn Bay, the starting-point for this walk is the seafront at Rhos. You could walk from there, or save 1 mile (½-mile out, ½-mile back) by using the car as I shall now describe.

From the centre of Rhos seafront, Rhos Road runs uphill past the shops and in about 700 yards reaches the traffic lights on the Llandudno-Colwyn Bay road, A546. Cross this main road and continue along the secondary road opposite. This soon comes to another crossroads, where the continuing road opposite is only a narrow lane with a gravel surface. Take the car 50 yards up this lane to where it widens near the entrance of an ancient quarry. Here the car can be turned and parked and the walk begins.

At the start of the narrow lane there are two signposts. One says BRYN EURYN and points up the lane, the other says LLYS EURYN and indicates a little footpath at the side of the lane. Go back a little way from where you leave the car and take the LLYS EURYN path. It's a narrow uphill path and you need to walk single-file between the thickets. After going along it for less than 5 minutes you come to all that is left of Llys Euryn — once Llys Rhos — a mediaeval hall built on the site of a Dark Ages palace. The ruins are overgrown with grass and creepers, but the tall old chimney still reaches high above the cavernous stone fireplace.

On your left as you face the fireplace there is a gap which allows you to get behind the ruined wall on that side. Here you'll find an intriguing little path that leads you safely round the rim of the ancient quarry, up past some pretty gardens, and under a

fallen tree into the narrow lane bound for Bryn Euryn. Turn right up the lane, and soon it curls to the left onto open grass slopes. From here a short steep path mounts to the summit of Bryn Euryn, where there is an Ordnance Survey cairn and a superb view.

The height is only 428 feet above the sea, but the splendid panorama over the River Conway, the Little Orme, and Colwyn Bay make it seem much loftier. Flower enthusiasts will notice (in summer) the limestone flora up here, including Rock Rose, Scabious, Harebell, and Traveller's Joy — common in southern England but rare in North Wales. You need to use some imagination to trace the blurred outlines of the hill fortress that occupied Bryn Euryn in primitive times; but anyone can see that it must have been an impregnable defensive position before the days of gunpowder.

For the descent, follow the broad track all the way down. It brings you straight to the car.

DEGANWY AND ITS CASTLE

ometime in the early centuries A.D. two holy women of Ireland, Modwenna and Bride, were sitting in a meadow close to the Irish shore with their servants Luge and Athea. Suddenly all four found themselves at sea — for the portion of the Emerald Isle they were on had broken away from the mainland. They floated eastward for a day and a night before their drifting island grounded on the shores of Britain at the mouth of a river. The river was the Conway, and the piece of Ireland (which quickly became part of the coast) was the peninsula of Deganwy.

Modwenna settled in Mercia, where as Saint Modwenna of the Forest of Arden she wrote the story of this miraculous journey. Saint Bride — or Sant Ffraidd, which is the Welsh form of her name — stayed in western Britain, and is commemorated by the village two miles farther up the estuary, Llansantffraidd Glan Conwy.

Many hundreds of years later the Norman conquerors of Britain built a castle on the rocky hill above Deganwy. For a long time Deganwy Castle was the limit of the Norman advance against the rebel Welsh princes, the object of fierce attacks and desperate defences. One of the first Norman lords to occupy it was Robert, Earl of Rhuddlan, who was sent there with a small force of men-at-arms to establish the Norman idea of law and order. One morning — it was July 3rd, 1088 — news reached the castle of a marauding force raiding from the mountains higher up the Conway. The Earl sent his tiny army to deal with it, under command of his lieutenant, while he himself remained in the castle with one knight and a few servants.

At noon of that day Robert of Rhuddlan 'was taking his midday sleep in the Castle, with no thought of danger or of warlike alarms,' when a frightened messenger toiled up to the castle gate to beg the Earl for help. Three ships, Welsh raiders from farther along the coast, were beached on the sands below Great Ormes Head. The men from them had seized women and cattle and were only waiting for the tide to carry them

41

off with their plunder. Earl Robert leaped from his bed and ordered all his retainers to follow him to the shore without a moment's delay. But when he rode sword in hand out of the gateway, wearing no armour, only his one knight followed him. They galloped down the steep path to the shore, came up to the three ships just as the tide was beginning to lift them, and demanded that the cattle and prisoners should be put ashore. The pirates replied with a shower of arrows and javelins. And Robert of Rhuddlan and his brave companion fell from their horses, dead.

For nearly two centuries after this event Deganwy Castle was attacked and defended, destroyed and rebuilt. Not until the year 1284, when King Edward 1 completed the building of Conway Castle on the opposite shore of the estuary, did the invading armies from England make much progress against the stubborn bravery of the Welsh. And by that time the little fortress on the rocky hill had fallen into disuse and was soon to become a ruin.

THE WALK :
TO DEGANWY CASTLE

MAP SQUARE C1
O.S. reference 782794
Easy. 1 hour. Care needed with small children in party.

Deganwy is five miles from Colwyn Bay via A55 and Llandudno Junction; a mile and a half from Conway, across the river bridge; and two miles from the centre of Llandudno, following Gloddaeth Road and the West Parade. There is a free car park at Deganwy immediately below the front of the Castle Hotel. Just above the Castle Hotel is York Road, turning off A496 to curve uphill. Go up this road for 5 minutes and look out for a PUBLIC FOOTPATH sign on the left. This marks the path to the Castle ruins. (The car could be brought as far as this, but it is preferable to leave it

in the authorised car park.)

The public footpath goes through a white gate onto open grassy hillside with crags above. If you expect to see a castle like those at Conway or Harlech, you'll be sadly disappointed. What you are visiting is a much older fortress; and what you are seeing is the ghost of a castle that was built here a thousand years ago.

The best way is to take the fortress in rear — go straight uphill, keeping the crags on your left, until an easy gap on that side, with a fragment of old wall on the right, enables you to mount into the grassy court or saddle between the rock horns. You can see now that this was a natural fortification. The turrets of crag on each side were there long before Man came, and all the Normans had to do was to build walls enclosing the space between the rock towers, and crown the towers themselves with stone battlements. The little crag on your left (if you enter as I've described) is easy to climb, by a narrow path. BUT I advise you to lead the way yourself and not to allow any small children to go up first. The summit is not very big, and drops in a sheer cliff from the farther edge.

There are no battlements left now, and what use the excavations and ledges were put to is anyone's guess. But the view alone (if the weather is clear) is worth the climb. Conway Castle and anchorage looks like a child's model, and among the Carnedd mountains that loom beyond is the second highest summit in Wales, Carnedd Llewelyn. Looking the other way, northward, Llandudno is spread like a town plan with Great Ormes Head protecting it like another and bigger fortress.

For the descent, go down from the crag by the same narrow path but turn left at the bottom. If you descend a little way from the 'courtyard', down grass slopes in the direction of Llandudno, you will quickly come to a narrow path running round the slopes. Go to the left along it. Soon the precipitous wall of the Castle crag appears above on your left, showing the largest area of man-made wall still remaining.

From the blocks of stone that lie half-buried beside the path below, it is easy to deduce what happened to the battlements.

The path finishes close to the gate of the public footpath, by which you regain York Road.

HOW PRINCE MADOC DISCOVERED AMERICA

wain Gwynedd, ruler of North Wales in the twelfth century, had nineteen sons. One of them was Idwal, whose story is told later in this book. Another was Madoc, who loved the sea better than the mountains of his own land. But the two princes of greatest importance were Howel and Dafydd, for Owain their father had resolved that between them they should rule Gwynedd after his death.

Owain died in December 1169; and the recorded date reminds us that he and his sons were historical persons. On his death Howel and Dafydd, like many other king's sons in history, quarrelled as to which should be the more powerful force in the kingdom and began a civil war, turning Gwynedd from a peaceful country into a land of strife. Now Prince Madoc was a peace-loving man, a thinker and a poet rather than a warrior. His courage and hardihood had been shown by several daring voyages, but he had no mind to win fame in battles, least of all by joining with Dafydd or Howel to fight against a brother. Each of the warring princes wished him to declare himself on their side, for Madoc was well loved by all who lived on the coasts of Gwynedd. To escape from this unhappy situation, Madoc determined to carry out an adventure he had long meditated. This was to sail westward beyond Ireland (where his brother Riryd had an estate) until he came to another land beyond the ocean, or — which was just as likely — until his ship met her fate in the unknown waters on the edge of the world.

So Prince Madoc at once rigged and manned the famous Gwennan Gorn, a ship of which little detail is known except that her planks were joined with stag's horns instead of nails and that Madoc had voyaged in her to distant islands in the northern sea. She was built of oak from the forests of Nant Gwynant, says one bard; and another, Gynfric ap Gronow, wrote :

> Gwennan Gorn, brought to the Gele
> To be given a new mast,
> Was taken then to the quay of Afon Ganol
> For Madoc's famous voyage.

For in those days the north coast of Gwynedd (where Colwyn Bay and Abergele stand today) had two small seaports at the river-mouths of the Gele and the Ganol. And from the quay of the Afon Ganol in the year 1170 the Gwennan Gorn sailed on her great venture.

It is recorded that Madoc's brother Riryd joined the ship at Lundy Island. Then she departed westward, and for several years nothing was heard of her. Then — and no one can be sure how long afterwards — the Gwennan Gorn came back. She had barely enough men on board to sail her, for all the rest had been left in the new land Madoc had discovered many weeks' sail across the western ocean. The Prince stayed in Gwynedd only long enough to gather a fleet of ten small ships and fill them with volunteers, both men and women, who would sail with him to the new land and make a new Gwynedd there.

The ten ships sailed, having collected at Lundy Island. And this time they were never heard of again . . . .

. . . . Unless the evidence of six hundred years later is to be believed. For during the seventeenth and eighteenth centuries, when the wilderness of North America was being opened up by the pioneers, reports began to come in of a large tribe of 'Red' Indians — the Mandans — whose skins were white and who spoke a language very similar to Welsh. This began a long period of exhaustive research which brought other old records to light; and on the testimony of these a great many people believe that Prince Madoc landed in Alabama in 1170, thus discovering North America more than 300 years before Columbus. And in 1953 a large memorial tablet was erected on the shore of Mobile Bay, Alabama, bearing these words :

> 'In memory of Prince Madoc, a Welsh explorer,
> who landed on the shores of Mobile Bay in 1170
> and left behind, with the Indians, the Welsh language.'

THE WALK :
TO THE QUAY FROM WHICH
MADOC SAILED FOR AMERICA

MAP SQUARE C1
O.S. reference 829815
Very easy pavement walking but
worth doing on foot. 1½ hours
out and back, including stops.

For this simple trip you need to know where to look rather than where to go. Nothing is the same as it was when Madoc sailed.

Start from Rhos-on-Sea. The free car park in Colwyn Avenue, just behind the sea-front, makes a good base. Turn right at exit from car park and in 200 yards you come to the Marine Drive and turn left with the open sea on your right. If you have to walk along a 'prom' the Rhos Marine Drive is as nice as any I know. Look out after 200 yards of it for what must be the smallest chapel in Wales, down on the right. A notice says :

> *Parish of Llandrillo-yn-Rhos*
> *All reverence is due to this sacred spot*
> *This ancient chapel*
> *is built over the holy well of Saint Trillo*
> *a Celtic saint of the sixth century*
> *Pilgrim turn in and offer prayer*
> *The Lord be with you.*

Even if you're not a pilgrim, don't fail to 'turn in' — it's worth a look, at least.

But for the memento of Madoc, walk on for another five minutes, with good views on your right of the Little Orme's Head jutting out beyond Penrhyn Bay. Soon you see the golf course on the landward side, opposite the raised pavement of the sea-front (for golfing fans, there's a grandstand view of the 9th-hole green from here). The last house before you come to the golf course is a big one, named Odstone. Looking into its garden, you see two ornamental pools. These are in what was once the river-bed of the Afon Ganol, where Madoc's ship lay alongside the quay. On the left as you look into the garden is a massive old wall or embankment of stone, now made into a rockery with the entrance drive running along its top. This is the old quay. There's an inscribed tablet on it, visible but not legible from the road. The garden is private, of course — so here is the inscription :

> *Prince Madoc sailed from here*
> *Aber-Kerrik-Gwynan, 1170 A.D.*
> *and landed at Mobile, Alabama*
> *with his ships*
> *Gorn Gwynant and Pedr Sant*

It will be noticed that this version speaks of two ships, and has a different spelling for 'Gwennan Gorn.' Still — now you've seen the actual place he sailed from, don't you feel that Prince Madoc may have beaten Columbus to it after all?

BANGOR AND MENAI

The Isle of St Seiriol

The lake that no bird will cross

The farmer who caught a fairy

THE ISLE OF ST SEIRIOL

o two Saints were ever more friendly than St Cybi and St Seiriol. Both these holy men lived on the Isle of Anglesey (Ongul's Ey as it was then called) in the sixth century; but Cybi lived in the north-west, where Holyhead now stands, and Seiriol lived in the extreme eastern corner nearly thirty miles away. It is told of them that for many years they met every day at the Wells of Clorach, halfway between Caer Gybi — where Cybi was building a church — and Penmon where Seiriol had his cell. Cybi walked fifteen miles south-eastward, with the sun of morning and noon on his face, and Seiriol walked fifteen miles north-westward with the sun behind him. When they parted to walk home again, the sun had crossed the sky. And as a consequence Cybi became dark and sunburned while Seiriol remained pale and fair. To this day they are called in Wales Cybi Felyn (Cybi of the Tawny Hue) and Seiriol Wyn (Seiriol the Fair).

In their later years these meetings ceased, for Cybi was increasingly devoted to his church in the north. So famous had the man and his work become that the northern headland was called Holy Head by the outlanders, though to the Welsh it was still known as Caergybi.

Seiriol, meanwhile, was equally renowned for his holiness and his inspired teaching. It is said that the Norse settlers who then inhabited much of Anglesey flocked to hear him speak and to be baptized, and no doubt as his fame spread the Saint was inconveniently besieged by daily crowds of disciples. He had his humble dwelling by a well (in time a Benedictine Priory was to be built here) but now Seiriol sought a more retired hermitage. Half-a-mile off-shore was a small island, and here he built himself another cell to which he could retreat when he wished to meditate apart from his followers. And so the island was given its first name — Priestholm — by the Norse Christians of Anglesey. Later, after Seiriol's death, it was named Ynys Seiriol by the Welsh; and later still the swarms of puffins — which still come here — earned it the

English name of Puffin Island.

Seiriol also had a chapel or hermitage on Penmaenmawr, five miles away beyond the shallows of what is now Conway Bay. And the ancient record that tells of this seems to confirm what some geologists hold to be true: that there was once a tract of sea-marsh and sand between Puffin Island and the mainland of Wales. 'This Seiriol' (says the document) 'hadd an hermytage at Penmaen Mawr, and there hadd a chappell where hee did bestowe much of his tyme in prayers . . . . and made from Priestholm to Penmaen Mawr a pavement whereupon hee might walke drye from his church at Priestholm to his chappell at Penmaen Mawr, the vale beynge very lowe grownde and wette, which pave^t may bee discerned from Penmaen Mawr to Priestholm when the sea is cleere, if a man liste to goe in a bote to see itt.'

Of St Seiriol's other accomplishments there is little record. Perhaps, though, it ranks as a very great achievement to be remembered in place-name and story for fourteen hundred years.

THE WALK: MAP SQUARE B1
TO ST SEIRIOL'S WELL AND   O.S. reference 631808
THE COAST BY PUFFIN ISLAND   Path, lane, sea-coast. Easy.
                                             1½-2 hours.

To reach the start of this little walk, get to the mainland end of the Menai Suspension Bridge first, and cross it — A5 — on to Anglesey; or, as a sign informs you: MON, MAM CYMRU ('Mona, Mother of Wales'). Turn sharp right at the island end of the bridge, on A545. A delightful 7-mile drive follows, through Menai Bridge village and Beaumaris. The ruined Beaumaris Castle, which you see close on the left as you pass through the little town, has a picturesque moat but no battles or sieges in its humdrum history. 1½ miles beyond Beaumaris look out for a right turn signposted PENMON 2. The curly lane brings you to another right-turn signpost — PRIORY, BLACK POINT — in about a mile, whence the lane runs right into the precincts of ancient Penmon Priory. (Car parking, 5p fee; by paying three times as much you can take the car right through to the coast, but you'll miss St Seiriol's Well if you do.)

The Priory buildings are interesting, and so is the huge dovecote on the right of the entrance gates beyond. Ministry of Works notices are there to tell you their history in brief. For the Well, go through the lane entrance and turn sharp left (signpost) on a narrow path. A stone doorway in a wall overgrown with massive ivy brings you to St Seiriol's Well, where the holy man used to baptize the converted heathen. The foundations of his cell are a few yards away on the left. On this side also an iron ladder-stile over the wall marks the start of a 20-minute pilgrimage which isn't signposted, to visit a stone cross 1,000 years old. Note that this is an out-and-back pilgrimage, returning past the Well.

Crossing the stile, continue 100 yards with an old limestone quarry face close on your right hand. You join a grassy track going uphill, and a short way up this you'll see the tall cross standing in the middle of a field. The notice beside it says that some of the much-worn carving on it is 'thought to represent the Temptation of St Anthony,' and this (to my mind) represents a remarkable flight of imagination on someone's part.

Retracing your steps past St Seiriol's Well to the lane by the entrance, turn left uphill and follow the lane over and down to the point — an easy 15-minute walk. The views are tremendous. From the shores of Black Point, where you'll find the Pilot House Restaurant, you look across half-a-mile of treacherous strait to Ynys Seiriol — or Priestholm, or Puffin Island — and its tower, reputed to stand where

Seiriol built one of his hermitages. Penmaenmawr, where he had a second hermitage, can be seen far away to the right; and we assume that Seiriol's causeway connecting the two is sunk below the intervening waters. If you 'list to goe in a bote to see itt,' you'll have to hire one at Beaumaris.

Limestone quarries prevent return along the coasts to left and right, but a small variant of the return route can be made. From opposite the lighthouse (whose solemn warning bell has a melodious chime) go left along the tops of the little cliffs — fine picnic places — for 5 minutes and then strike uphill on the crest of a low-relief limestone ridge, thus regaining the lane 10 minutes' walk from the car.

THE LAKE THAT NO BIRD WILL CROSS

In the year 1140 Owain, son of Cynan, was Prince of Gwynedd, a country corresponding to the modern Caernarfonshire and Merionethshire. Owain Gwynedd, as he was called, had nineteen sons, and one of them named Idwal was a very beautiful child. At the time when Idwal was a young boy the Prince of Gwynedd was engaged in a fierce war with Howel King of Powys, and as there was a possibility that the forces of Powys would make murderous foray into Gwynedd, Owain resolved to find some place of safety where Idwal could be hidden. At the same time, he wished to have the boy educated in the arts of poetry and the harp.

After taking the advice of his counsellors and friends, to no avail, he remembered a distant relative who lived in a small mansion in the midst of the craggy wilderness not far from St Curig's Chapel. Nefydd was this man's name, and Owain recalled that he was a bard and harpist of no common order. So young Idwal was sent as foster-son to Nefydd, to live and be instructed among the huge peaks that stand around Llyn Ogwen.

Now this Nefydd was a very handsome man who had grown vainer with the years, so that he called himself Nefydd Hardd — Nefydd the Beautiful. He had a son of Idwal's age, named Dunawt. It was another of Nefydd's vanities to boast that Dunawt would grow up as beautiful as himself, though in fact Dunawt was a very plain youth and as dull in mind as he was homely in countenance. When he and Idwal sat together, as they often did while Nefydd gave them instruction, no one — not even a vain and wilfully blind father — could fail to see that Idwal was incomparably the better-looking of the two. And it was very quickly made clear to Dunawt that his foster-brother was far more clever than he could ever be.

As the days passed into weeks and the weeks into months, the envy and jealousy of both father and son smouldered more hotly until at last it burst into flame. Taking Dunawt aside, Nefydd suggested that he should lead Idwal into one of the wild mountain recesses to show him the lake that lay there beneath some of the grimmest precipices in Cambria.

'By its west shore the water is deep,' he added. 'If Prince Idwal were to fall in, Dunawt, he would drown, for neither he nor you are able to swim.'

Dunawt was not so dull but he could understand what was proposed. He and Idwal set off up the mountainside and came to the big and gloomy lake between the precipices. They walked along the stony strand and then along the west shore, where smooth rocks overhung the water. A brutal thrust, a few moments of helpless agony, and the thing was done.

When the report of Idwal's death reached Owain Gwynedd he caused inquiry to be made, as a result of which it appeared certain that Idwal had been murdered at Nefydd's order. But the deed could not be proved against him. The Prince of Gwynedd then decreed that Nefydd and his posterity should be degraded from their rank of gentlemen and be bondsmen for ever.

As for the lake where his handsome son was drowned, it was called Llyn Idwal from that time forth, and because of the foul deed that was done there no bird will fly across its dark waters.

THE WALK;
TO LLYN IDWAL

MAP SQUARE B2
O.S. reference 645595
Rough track, magnificent
scenery. 20 minutes to lake.

The walk starts from the top of the Nant Ffrancon pass, at the western end of Llyn Ogwen. This point is just over 9 miles from Bangor on the A5, at a Mountain Centre (Ogwen Cottage) and Rescue Post where the main road reaches 993 feet

57

above sea-level. It's probably best to park a short distance along the lakeside and walk back to the Mountain Centre, which is maintained by the City of Birmingham. At the west side of the building note a Public Footpath sign in Welsh and English; Llwybyr Cyhoeddus, the Welsh form, is often taken by visitors to signify TOILETS, with sometimes embarrassing consequences.

Follow the direction of the sign, past the building, up a rocky incline, and through a gate. The broad and very stony path beyond mounts gently over open hillside, gradually entering the jaws of a great dent in the flank of the Glyder range of mountains. In about half a mile you pass through another gate and stand at the end of the lake, with Cwm Idwal's giant walls rising round you.

Nowhere in the British Isles can the heart of wild mountains be reached so easily. Llyn Idwal is popular with climbers, walkers, and nature students, but its many visitors can't spoil its grandeur. Y Garn towers above on the right, Glyder Fawr on the left, both mountains over 3,000 feet. The line of cliffs above the farther end of the lake is split down the centre by the giant cleft called the Devil's Kitchen. On your left as you face in this direction are the smaller crags known as the Gribin Facet, where you'll probably see rock-climbers engaged in their sport. The Idwal Slabs, a classic climbing ground, are farther away beyond the head of the lake.

It's possible to walk right round the lake. But in any but the driest weather you're likely to cross boggy bits — fair enough in mountain boots but not in ordinary shoes. My guess is that Dunawt administered the fatal push to Idwal over on your right, where a grey wall of rock drops steeply into the lake. It's a good place to swim from — or to sit and keep watch for any lake-crossing birds who haven't heard of the legend.

THE FARMER WHO CAUGHT A FAIRY

he young farmer of Ystrad, the farm under the sheep-pastures of Moel Eilio, discovered where the fairy maidens used to dance on moonlit nights. It was a small field between the farmhouse and the river. One night he was in his usual hiding-place, watching them, when the most beautiful of them all danced very near to where he was hidden. He sprang out, caught her up in his arms, and ran with her to the house. With shrill cries of despair the rest of the fairies vanished.

The captured fairy was well treated although she was firmly held prisoner, for the young farmer was deep in love with her and wished her to marry him. But for all his protestations she would grant him nothing. At last she told him that she would be his servant, but only if he could guess what her name was. He tried all the girls' names he could think of, but in vain. Then he bethought him of the dancing-place, and hid himself there once more. As he had hoped, the fairy maidens were dancing that night, and talking together as they danced.

'If only she could be with us!' he heard one of them sigh. 'But she is a prisoner of the humans. Alas, poor Penelope!'

If he had tried for a hundred years the young farmer would never have guessed that name, but now he had it. Hurrying to the house, he greeted the fairy maiden triumphantly by her name, and once more asked her to marry him. Still she would not, though she now undertook to be his servant as she had agreed. With this he had to be content — and indeed there was soon no more contented farmer in all Gwynedd. Everything prospered for him and his fairy servant. The cows gave a full milking three times a day, the flocks and herds multiplied with magical speed, and in a year he was farming (besides his own freehold of Ystrad) all the lands on the north side of Nant-y-Bettws to the top of Snowdon and all Cwmbrwynog in Llanberis, an extent of 5,000 acres.

Every night and morning the young farmer asked the fairy maiden to marry him. And at last she consented, with just one condition.

'You must never, never strike me with iron,' she told him. 'If that happens, I must leave you for ever and return to my own people.'

He laughed at that strange condition, for such a blow could not pass between him and his true love. So they were married, and lived happily for several years. Then, one day, the young farmer went to the field to catch the pony, for he and his wife intended to ride to Caernarfon fair that day. The fairy wife went to help him. The pony was mischievous and would not come near the man who held the bridle and bit in his hand, and when the beast had played his tricks for a while the man lost his temper and hurled the bridle at him. It missed the pony and struck his wife.

The instant she felt the cold iron on her cheek she vanished. The last the husband knew of her was a wailing voice, very faint and growing fainter, imploring him to look after their children.

That was the end of the farmer's fairy marriage, but the children of the fairy Penelope grew up and had children of their own. The people of that valley had never been able to get their tongues round the fairy wife's strange name and turned Penelope into Pelling, and now her descendants were called Pellings. As long afterwards as the nineteenth century there were highly-respected Welsh folk who claimed fairy blood, and declared proudly that they were descended from the Pellings of Ystrad.

THE WALK:
TO THE MEADOWS OF YSTRAD
AND NANT MILL WATERFALL

MAP SQUARE B2
O.S. reference 535576
Easy path across fields, pretty
river garden. About 1½ hours.

Caernarfon is the setting-out place for this expedition. Take A4085, the Beddgelert road, passing through Waunfawr. Five miles from Caernarfon you cross a bridge over the little river Gwyrfai, and just beyond it on the left you'll see the church of Betws Garmon. Stop here (roadside parking) opposite a licensed farm-restaurant which has a small caravan park nearby.

The most pleasant way of doing this very short and easy walk is for the car to meet the walkers at the other end, one mile farther along the road where there is a small layby on the right. However, on a sunny day the walk there-and-back by the footpath is enjoyable enough.

There is a green Public Footpath sign beside the buildings of the farm-restaurant. Go through the gate below it, and through the second gate, beyond which is a bridge that once crossed the old narrow-gauge line of the Welsh Highland railway. Don't cross this bridge, but turn left and in 40 paces reach a third gate on the left. Go through this. In about 100 yards you can step through the fence on the left and walk along the old rail track, now a grassy path.

The 'small field between the farmhouse and the river' where the fairies used to dance must have been somewhere here, for if you look across to the left you'll see the old farmhouse of Ystrad a little way up the slopes of Moel Eilio, with trees round it. You can also see, higher up and to the left, the gaping shafts of the disused mines, whose opening no doubt chased away the last fairy from Ystrad.

Soon you cross Afon Gwyrfai by an iron railway bridge from which you can look down into the clear water and (perhaps) see brown trout or even a salmon. Ahead the flat river meadows begin to narrow. You pass in front of a house, then along a straight stretch of stone embankment. Just above on the right there is a moss-grown 'strongpoint,' relic of the invasion fears of World War Two; young explorers usually find this exciting. Go under the bridge beyond, stepping over a barrier, and at once turn left, with a step over a wire fence. This brings you in a few yards to a lane and a very old bridge crossing the river. Down on your left are the gardens of the Nant Mill waterfall, miniature indeed but really charming. When you emerge on the main road in a few more paces (the layby already mentioned is to your right) turn left, and you can enter the gardens.

A notice on the gate says 'PRIVATE, BUT YOU ARE INVITED TO PASS THROUGH,' and the word Welcome is set in white pebbles on the path. In these days of access squabbles and enclosure of National Park land it's a heartening thing to find a private owner opening his land freely to visitors. The foaming river and the pretty paths are not the only attractions here. A famous sight from May onwards are the elvers, immature eels, here to be seen wriggling up the waterfall on their way to Cwellyn Lake, after (believe it or not) a 3-year journey from the Sargasso Sea where they were born.

If you walk back to the starting-point, do so by the same route and not by the road, which is unsafe for walkers in the holiday season. If a car is in the layby to meet you, you could drive on along the shore of Cwellyn Lake — only ½-mile from Nant Mill waterfall — where there are places for a picnic.

LLEYN AND TREMADOC BAY
The rising of the lark
Helen's spring
The Accursed Village

hey say that when David Owen, a young and gifted Bard, lay dying, he called for his harp, saying that he had just heard one of the sweetest songs of heaven. The harp was brought. And in the short time before he died the harpist played the famous tune Dafydd y Garreg Wen, 'David of the White Rock,' to which in after years Sir Walter Scott wrote the English words. That was in the year 1749, and David Owen was then 29 years old. A less melancholy story is told of his earlier years, and concerns another of his famous compositions.

The name 'Borth-y-Gest' signifies 'the port of the land of Gest'; for the district westward along the coast from the mouth of the Glaslyn river was called Gest. In the eighteenth century small coasting vessels plied to and from Borth-y-gest, many of them hailing from France or Spain and carrying wines and silks, tobacco and spirits — cargoes that would show a very handsome profit if they could be sold without passing through the Customs. (Some of this contraband, it is said, found its way as far inland as Chirk, where it stocked the cellars of the great Sir Watkin Wynn.) In these days there lived at Borth-y-gest a retired sea-captain named Captain Williams, who grew fat on the profit from the contraband trade and was always known as Captain Williams the Smuggler. The Smuggler's house, Plas-y-Borth, was more like a tavern than a private house on most evenings, for he loved to hold a noson lawen, a 'merry evening,' at which there would be music and dancing, and the wine and cwrw da (good ale) would flow freely. The heart and soul of the noson lawen was David Owen, the young harpist and composer of songs.

David's home was the farm Y Garreg Wen, so named from the big pale-coloured rock that stood solitary on the hill just above it. The hill was between the farmhouse and the little port, and David was accustomed to walk that way on his visits to the Smuggler's house. One night in late Spring the noson lawen at Plas-y-Borth was over and David Owen was making his way back home by the familiar path over the hill. There had been song after song, and dance after dance, until the harpist's fingers were weary; but his skill had won him clamorous applause — and innumerable mugs of ale provided by his admirers. Indeed, his cargo of cwrw da impelled David to lie down and go to sleep, though he had reached the top of the hill and had only a few hundred yards to go to reach the farmhouse.

When he woke it was near sunrise of a May morning. He was lying on the dewy grass close to the side of the White Rock, with the distant mountains ranged against the glowing east. High above his head a lark, its wings tipped with golden light, was carrying its song far into the misty blue of the sky. In that moment of wonder David conceived the melody and words of Codiad yr Ehedydd, 'The Rising of the Lark,' a song whose gaiety and tunefulness quickly made it popular through all Wales. You will hear it sung at a noson lawen today. And it was adopted as the regimental march of the Welsh Guards.

THE WALK:
TO THE WHITE ROCK

MAP SQUARE B3
O.S. reference 560374
Moderately short and easy. 1 hour, or 1½ if extended as suggested.

Borth-y-gest, from which this walk starts, is less than a mile from Portmadoc, with delightful sandy coves (care needed with children bathing) just beyond the small bay. No through road. Leave the car in the car park (fee for parking) on the west side of the bay, and walk from the car park entrance up the steep hill of Mersey Street, which has a shop and post office on the right near the bottom and the village

school at the top. When you are nearly at the top, turn right, with the wall of the school playground on your left. The broad lane turns sharply left round the corner of a school annexe and becomes a narrow path, between bushes and then up a brackeny hillside. It leads to a stone wall with a large wooden gate, padlocked. For some time it has been intended to erect a stile here and by the time you reach the spot one may have been provided. In any case, it is easy to climb over the gate; which, incidentally, commands a glimpse of the open sea on the left.

Beyond the gate, take the faint path that goes straight on for 100 yards to strike a broad curving track connecting caravan emplacements. Turn left up this, and in a dozen paces you will see, close on your right, a wooden stile crossing a barbed-wire fence. Go over the stile. The White Rock is 50 yards ahead on the open green hill-crest.

The view from the Garreg Wen is worth more than a quick glance. If it is clear, you can see the Lleyn Peninsula and the Rivals; Moel Hebog; Moel Ddu and the shoulder of Lliwedd above the wooded hill on the north; the tip of Cnicht, and the Moelwyns; Borth-y-gest below with Manod Mawr and the Ffestiniog valley beyond; and across the estuary the Rhinog range with Harlech Castle below. There used to be a tablet on the White Rock inscribed with the opening line of David Owen's song — Cwyd, cwyd, ehedydd, cwyd — but some years ago it was destroyed by vandals.

To vary the return route, try the slightly longer way that follows. Go back over the stile to the broad caravan track and turn to the right along it — Criccieth Castle is seen straight ahead, four miles distant — but only walk for a few paces. You will see, sharp on your left, half-a-dozen caravans in a small glen. Go down the glen between the caravans. There is a lookout rock with a fine sea view at its lower end, and from below this a steep and narrow path drops down through the thickets to emerge on a broad lane opposite a cottage gate with the name BORTH FECHAN.

Turn left along this lane for 50 paces, then turn right down another narrow path heading for the coast. Bear left when this forks. You will quickly come to the Beach Cafe and the coastal path that runs above the Borth-y-gest beaches. Turn left along this path and you can reach the car park in 10 minutes.

HELEN'S SPRING

t is related that in the fourth century A.D. the Roman legions in Britain were commanded by Magnus Maximus, who in defiance of Rome declared himself Emperor of Britain. In the Roman city of Segontium, which stood where Caernarfon now stands, the Emperor Maximus wooed and won the beautiful Welsh princess Elen, afterwards known as Queen Helen of the Hosts because of her fondness for marching with her husband's legions. Helen was anxious that her countrymen throughout all Wales should be able to communicate freely with each other, and to this end she persuaded the Emperor to construct a paved road through the mountains from north to south of the country. Parts of that road were to endure for fifteen hundred years, known to the Welsh as Sarn Elen, or Helen's Causeway; and as Sarn Elen it appears on the Ordnance Survey maps of the twentieth century.

Queen Helen had two sons, both of whom grew up to hold command in the Emperor's army. Her favourite was the younger. One day Helen was journeying southward from Segontium with a large escort of legionaries, passing Llyn Cwellyn and marching thence through the Pass of Aberglaslyn in the direction of Ffestiniog. A separate body of soldiers followed some distance behind, as a rearguard. This rearguard was commanded by Helen's younger son.

Beyond Aberglaslyn the Roman road climbed from Nantmor over the foot of Cnicht. Then, as now, it was a toilsome ascent, and when the Queen's party reached a spring a little way down on the other side Helen sat down to rest and drink the pure cold water. While she was still resting here, a breathless man came clattering down the stony trail, bringing tragic news from the rearguard.

What had happened was this: the track along the shore of Cwellyn lake passed below a grim crag called Castell Cidwm, where the giant Cidwm was reputed to live as in a fortress. No sign of the giant had been seen by Helen and her escort, and they had journeyed on unmolested. But as the rearguard came beneath the frowning precipice an arrow – presumably shot by Cidwm – had sped down from the crags and killed Helen's favourite son.

There were many who whispered, afterwards, that it was the jealous elder brother who had shot the arrow, trusting that the fabled giant of the crag would be blamed. Perhaps Queen Helen herself suspected that this might be the terrible truth, for a great cry broke from her in her native tongue: 'Croes awr – croes awr i mi!' ('Cursed hour – cursed hour to me!') And from this cry the spot took its name of Croesawr or Croesor; so that when – centuries later – a small village sprang up near Ffynnon Elen, as the spring was called, the name Croesor was transferred to the village. And both Croesor and Ffynnon Elen are there at the foot of Cnicht mountain, overlooking Traeth Mawr, to this day.

THE WALK:
TO FFYNNON ELEN

MAP SQUARE B2
O.S. reference 629448
Short and easy. ½-hour – but worth extending for a picnic.

To reach the village of Croesor by car from Portmadoc, take A498 as if for Beddgelert but turn right on B4410 two miles beyond Tremadoc. This joins A4085 at the village of Garreg. Turn left at the junction, through the village, and look out for a mediaeval-seeming archway on the right rather less than ¼-mile from the junction. (There is a signpost, Croesor.) Turn right here and follow the charming uphill lane, narrow but with passing-places, for 2½ miles. At the top of a steep hill the village appears suddenly on the left, and is reached by turning left at a crossroads of lanes.

If driving from the north (Beddgelert) direction, turn left across Aberglaslyn bridge and left again when you reach the archway three miles farther on.

The car can be left in Croesor village, which has no motorable through road. A lane turns off below the conspicuous chapel, heading towards a pointed mountain in the distance — Cnicht; the village post office is on the corner of this lane. Go along it for 30 yards, then go through an iron gate on the left that leads to a green slope between the cottages.The slope soon narrows to a pathway curling round a knoll into a small field. Cross the field to a gap in the wall, by an iron gate, and turn right, on a stony lane beneath trees. (The animal drinking-trough in the field is supplied from Ffynnon Elen.) A little iron gate on the right guards a sunken water-tank, put there when the old spring was diverted to make a water supply for Croesor village. Go on 36 yards past the gate, and in the wall on your left you will see the mossy mouth of the spring from which Queen Helen of the Hosts drank long ago.

In dry weather no water flows here now; the diversion has sent the flow of the spring underground, and only after plenty of rain does the small mossy opening show itself as an active ffynnon.

You could return to the car in 10 minutes by going back to the gap in the wall and instead of turning through it taking the metalled lane beyond the iron gate. But this short walk is well worth extending by continuing up the stony track beyond Helen's Spring. In 5 minutes or a little more you emerge on a miniature pass, with a grand view of Moel Hebog, the Eifionydd mountains, and — nearer on your right — the heathery crags of Yr Arddu. You could picnic near here. Or, better still, go on for another 10 minutes along the same track, downhill to an ideal picnic spot by the little river Dylif, where a bridge of huge stone slabs crosses the water.

THE ACCURSED VILLAGE

very long time ago three holy men, barefooted monks from the neighbourhood of St Beuno's shrine, clambered down the craggy defile leading to Nant Gwrtheyrn, intending to preach the Christian gospel to the villagers in the remote hamlet at the sea's edge. Now the chief man of Nant Gwrtheyrn village was a pagan, and he would have none of the monk's gospel. Instead, he and his henchmen drove the three holy ones with stones and curses back up the glen to its precipitous rim. Then it was the turn of the monks for cursing, and each of them placed his own curse on the village at the foot of the glen. No one who was born in the village, cried one monk, should ever lie in consecrated ground after death. No male and female born therein should ever be able to marry each other, said another. And the third monk declared that at last the village of Nant Gwrtheyrn would decay and die, to become for ever a deserted ruin.

The years and the generations passed, and time showed that the first two of these curses, at least, were effective. The men of Nant Gwrtheyrn, who were mostly fishermen, died by drowning or by falling from the cliffs into deep water, and their bodies were not recovered. By similar chances the women, too, failed to achieve burial in the only consecrated ground in those parts, namely, St Beuno's churchyard at Clynnog. By now they were all Christians at Nant Gwrtheyrn, and the women — fearful of the curses — customarily left the village when they were of an age to marry; while the men sought their wives from places outside the valley.

There came a time, two or three hundred years ago, when a youth and a maiden who had both been born in the village resolved to defy the curse and marry. All went well at first. The two exchanged presents on their wedding-morning (the bride's present to her man was a puppy-dog) and the sun shone brightly down through the branches of the ancient oaks which then grew near the village. The old tradition was followed — that the bride should feign bashfulness and hide herself, so that the bridegroom and his friends could seek her out and carry her off to the church. But when the groom's party came to look for the girl she was not to be found. They hallooed, they sought for hours. At nightfall she was still missing. Next day the distracted bridegroom and all the villagers sought high and low; and the next day; and the next. But she was gone, and for ever. It was thought she had fallen from the cliffs into the sea, and was drowned, so that the curse should remain unbroken.

The poor bridegroom, broken-hearted and bereft of reason, paced every day up and down the shore with the dog, her wedding gift, in his arms. Month by month, year by year, he spent his time in this way; until the people of the village discovered that the dog he had carried about for so long was dead. They flung the body into the sea. And next day the man, too, was gone — drowned.

The years passed, but the tragic story was still remembered in Nant Gwrtheyrn. There came a night of terrible storm, with lightning smiting the cliffs above the village and rocks crashing down. A thunderbolt struck one of the old oaks near the village, splitting it open. In the morning, when the folk came to look at it, they saw that the tree had been hollow, and that a skeleton was gripped, as in a vice, by the narrow depths of that hollow trunk: a skeleton with long silky har. They knew, then, where the bride in the old story had hidden herself.

The skeleton was placed reverently in a coffin, and a horse was harnessed to drag it up the precipitous ascent so that it could be taken to St Beuno's church for burial. But at the very top of the ascent, where the path ran along the cliff edge, the horse stumbled and fell down the precipice. The coffin was smashed into matchwood. And the bones of that skeleton were so scattered and lost among the boulders that there was no possibility of burial in ground consecrated or unconsecrated.

Still the years passed. Roads and quarries brought new life to the north coast under the heights of Yr Eifl, and a thriving new village sprang up in Nant Gwrtheyrn. There were fine stone cottages, fertile gardens, a school, and a chapel. When the nineteenth century turned into the twentieth this was a happy community, fortunately situated and caring little for the old dark legends of centuries gone by. What, then, of the third curse?

Go to Nant Gwrtheyrn today, and see. The fine stone cottages, the school, the chapel, the gardens — they are still there; the gardens all brambles and nettles, the buildings all broken and uninhabited. The curse of the third monk has come upon Nant Gwrtheyrn, and it is a dead village, a deserted ruin.

THE WALK:
TO NANT GWRTHEYRN

MAP SQUARE A2
O.S. reference 350450
Good track but very steep. 900 feet to go down and come up again. Leave high heels and the Under Eights in the car.

The village of Llithfaen, on the southern slopes of the Rivals (Yr Eifl, their Welsh name, means 'the fork') is the first objective for this walk. To reach it from Portmadoc and Criccieth, follow A497 through Llanystumdwy but bear right 1¼ miles farther on, taking B4354 through Chwilog to Four Crosses where you keep straight on across A499. From Pwllheli, leave the town on A499 and at Four Crosses (3 miles) turn left on B4354. Three miles beyond Four Crosses is a crossroads where Llithfaen is signposted, to the left on a minor road heading towards the bold shapes of the Rivals. Two and a half miles of this bring you uphill to Llithfaen; keep straight on over the village crossroads, steeply uphill. The lane, unfenced now,

emerges on heathery slopes above the sea ½-mile beyond Llithfaen. A right fork mounts along the hillside, but take the short left fork to an obvious parking-place on the left of the lane, and leave the car here. You are 922 feet above sea-level. The highest peak of the Rivals, 1,949 feet, rises above and you may just make out, on its summit, part of the Iron Age hill-fort called Tre'r Ceiri, the Town of the Giants. Walk on from the parking-place, downhill, through a gateway with a cattle-grid in it, and Nant Gwrtheyrn opens quite suddenly below you.

At the first corner of the steep descent it is clear that the notice higher up — UNSUITABLE FOR MOTORS — is no exaggeration! Except from the sea and the beach, this is the only approach to the deep glen below and that could be the real reason why the village is uninhabited today. In 20 minutes you are down at the village, and as you approach it the place looks (like the farmhouse higher up) as though it is lived in and cared for. A few paces nearer, and you perceive that the sturdy stone cottages are windowless and desolate. The chapel — Seilo — bears the date 1878. In 1948 there was still a congregation here on Sundays, and children attending the village school. Then the quarrymen and their families left, and only one cottage remained inhabited — by the coastguard. A dozen years ago he, too, found another home; and the only inhabitants since then have been the 'hippies' who made Nant Gwrtheyrn their temporary residence in 1970.

Only the disused quarries and their debris prevent the glen from being both scenic and charming. As it is, the beach — 5 minutes below the village — gives excellent bathing and there are good picnic spots.

It took one middle-aged couple 35 minutes to get up again from the village to the car.

SNOWDON

The story of Gelert

King Arthur's last battle

Glendower's chimney

THE STORY OF GELERT

lewelyn, the son of Iorwerth Drwyndwn, was a Prince of Wales in the twelfth century, a man as renowned for his skill in battle as for his delight in hunting. In summer he would often reside with his family in a hunting lodge at the foot of Snowdon, near where the village of Beddgelert now stands. He had many dogs, but his favourite was Gelert, who was not only courageous in hunting the boar and the wolf but also a friend of the whole family — 'a lamb at home, a lion in the chase.'

One day the Prince and his Princess went out hunting with their followers, leaving their baby son in charge of a nurse and one servant. The nurse, as it turned out, was a scatterbrain unworthy of trust, for no sooner had her master and mistress ridden away to the sound of cheerful noises from the huntsman's horn than she and the servant went off for a walk on the hills. The baby, son and heir to Prince Llewelyn, was left in his cradle, quite alone.

Meanwhile the hunt ranged far and wide, until it was noticed that Gelert was no longer among the dogs. The Prince was uneasy. Gelert was always foremost on the scent and first into the attack. Why had he abandoned the party — and where would he go, except back to the house? Llewelyn commanded an end to the chase and bade his followers return with him and his wife. They rode swiftly back and reached the hunting-lodge. And as they were dismounting, Gelert came running out of the house, covered with blood and wagging his tail.

The Princess, shrieking the name of her child, swooned away. Llewelyn rushed into the room where the baby had been — to find the cradle overturned, the bed-clothes piled in a bloodstained heap, and no sign of his infant son. It seemed to him that the dog must have killed the child. Blind with sorrow and fury, he drew his sword and drove it through poor Gelert, who gave a piercing yell as he died. Like a small echo, there came a shrill crying from beneath the cradle. One of the Prince's followers lifted the cradle, and there beneath it, quite unhurt, was the baby. Then Llewelyn pulled aside the pile of bedclothes, revealing the lifeless carcass of an enormous wolf, terrible even in death.

The Prince wept tears of remorse at this discovery. He owed his child's life to Gelert's keen instinct and courage, and he had rewarded the faithful dog with a fatal sword-stroke. Resolving that Gelert should be remembered as long as there were men and dogs on this earth, he caused the dog to be buried in a green meadow nearby, and the place marked with stones and shown to all who came.

A village sprang up in later years, and this was called Bedd Gelert, the Grave of Gelert. And eight hundred years after Prince Llewelyn's over-hasty deed there may still be found, every year, a few visitors who fulfil his wish :

> 'A pious monument I'll rear
> In memory of the brave;
> And passers-by will drop a tear
> On faithful Gelert's grave.'

THE WALK:
TO GELERT'S GRAVE

MAP SQUARE : B2
O.S. reference 592478
Short and easy. 45 minutes; or
1½ hours if extended.

Beddgelert is at the junction of A487 and A498, 4 miles south of Snowdon. The free car park is close to the Royal Goat Hotel, where A498 heads south from the village towards Portmadoc. Park the car here, and turn left at the car park entrance to walk down through the village to the bridge by which the road crosses the River Colwyn. Turn right immediately before the bridge, along a broad lane that has the river on its left just beyond the wall. This lane quickly ends at a footbridge crossing the River Glaslyn (into which the Colwyn stream flows here) with a small gate on the right, before you step onto the footbridge, signposted TO GELERT'S GRAVE.

Through the small gate is a delightful path following the riverside downstream, under trees. After going along it for 250 yards take the path on the right — the only one — running straight between wire fences and leading to the grave of Gelert, which can be seen from the turning. Beneath a small sycamore tree, fenced by railings, is a large slate slab inscribed with a brief version of the legend.

Modern research has discredited the story of Gelert, and prefers the theory that the village is named for a saint or hermit called Kelert, who was buried near here. However, archaeologists are quite often wrong. And as you read the words carved on the slab you will probably find yourself deciding that this really is the grave of poor Gelert — even if you don't drop a tear on it.

This very short walk is well worth extending. Return as far as the river bank and there turn right, downstream, along the bank of the Glaslyn. This is a public right-of-way. In 10 minutes you come to the iron girder bridge by which the old narrow-gauge Welsh Highland Railway used to cross the river. Cross this (it is a footbridge now) and turn left on the other side, to follow the river upstream by its true left bank. There are many good picnic places on this side. If not stopping for lunch, allow about 20 minutes for the walk from the girder bridge to the footbridge, which you cross to the GELERT'S GRAVE signpost where you started the footpath part of the walk. From here to the car park is 5-10 minutes.

The extended walk could be rewarding for any bird-lover who keeps his eyes open. The last time I did it was in mid-September, and I spotted heron, grey wagtail, dipper, and (believe it or not) a goldcrest, smallest of all European birds.

KING ARTHUR'S LAST BATTLE

he great days of the Round Table were over. Arthur and his knights had succeeded in driving the pagan Saxons back into England, and the mailed champions who had charged under the Red Dragon banner were dispersed. King Arthur himself was no longer young; and there were those, among them the treacherous Sir Modred, who whispered that it was time a new king ruled in Britain. Modred sent a message secretly to the leader of the Saxons, in eastern England, appointing a meeting-place in the mountains of North Wales. If the Saxon army would join him there, he said, he would raise a second army and together they would make an end of King Arthur and his power.

Arthur was in his palace at Caerleon-upon-Usk when news of the renewed Saxon invasion was brought to him. Swiftly he gathered as many of his knights as he could find, including the faithful Sir Bedivere who had never left him, and marched northward. When he reached Dinas Emrys, a mile beyond Beddgelert up the Gwynant valley, a man of the valley told him that the great host of Saeson was encamped beneath the walls of the old city of Tregalan, in the upper part of Cwm Llan. So King Arthur and the remnant of his chivalry advanced up this deep valley that lies under the central summit of Snowdon.

The battle that followed lasted all that day. It was a winter's day, and from grey morning to grey evening the clash of steel and the battle-shout and the moans and screams of wounded men filled the wide cwm and echoed dismally from its crags. Hour by hour, foot by foot, the King's warriors forced their enemies farther into the cwm, and up the rocky hillside towards the crest of the precipice between Snowdon and Lliwedd. At nightfall the struggle had reached the crest. But it was a small and weary struggle now, for very few men were left alive. And here, in the gathering darkness of winter, King Arthur met his death.

Some say that a chance arrow slew Arthur, one of a last volley shot by the Saxons; and that Bwlch-y-Saethau, the Pass of the Arrows, was so called because of it. Others say that it was Modred himself that killed the King. Both, it seems, were sorely wounded when they met in the twilight on Bwlch-y-Saethau. Modred got in his blow first, and it was a death-blow. But Arthur lifted his own sword, Excalibur, and with one last great stroke clove through steel helm and skull and brain. Modred fell. And Arthur, near to death, fell beside him.

Then Sir Bedivere carried him precariously down the crags to the shores of Llydaw, and there a black barge, wherein sat three beautiful women, waited. The dying King was borne away into the night mist, while such of his warriors as survived the battle made their way into a cave on the precipice-face of Lliwedd, there to await the second coming of their royal leader.

THE WALK:
TO LLYN LLYDAW

MAP SQUARE B2
O.S. reference 628544
Easy. About 3 miles out and back. Allow 2 hours.

The top of the Llanberis Pass is on A4086, six miles from Llanberis and five miles from Capel Curig. From Beddgelert, following A498 and turning left at Pen-y-gwryd, the distance is nine miles. There is a large car park (fee) but it is as well to get there early at holiday time because the cars of those starting out to climb Snowdon are parked here. This walk, on a broad track all the way, takes you as far into the heart of Snowdon as you can reasonably go without proper boots and clothing for mountains.

From the car park (near which there is a restaurant) follow the wide, gently-

climbing track across the mountainside. There are sure to be other people on it, for this is the Miners' Path that leads to the ascent of Snowdon by 'The Zigzags,' above Glaslyn. The track gives a downward glimpse of the upper Gwynant valley before it curls round the flank on the right. Now it descends slightly past a small lake, Llyn Teyrn, beside which you see the ruins of the tiny houses where the men who worked the old copper-mines of Snowdon used to live, going home at weekends. Beyond Llyn Teyrn it climbs again, still curving into the high glen walled by steep mountains that slowly opens ahead. When you come to Llyn Llydaw you see one of the grandest of all views of Snowdon summit, for Yr Wyddfa — as the highest point in England and Wales is called — rises magnificently beyond the far end of the lake.

The track goes to the right, crossing an arm of the lake by a stone causeway. (In winter, or after very heavy rain, the causeway may be partly under water.) Follow the track round the lake shore past the old copper mine and halt where it begins to climb steeply from the waterside. This is your terminus, for the return is made by the same route. And from here you can see the setting for the final acts of the King Arthur legend.

The huge precipice of Lliwedd looms opposite across the lake; its crest is 2,947 feet above sea-level. The lower crest to the right of it, separating it from the upsurge of Snowdon summit, is Bwlch-y-Saethau, the Pass of the Arrows, where the heathen hordes were driven back over the edge and where Arthur and Modred fought their last fight. It must have been by that precipitous way down the ridge to your right that Bedivere carried his dying master to the lake shore and the waiting barge, for the crags under Bwlch-y-Saethau are too steep for such work.

As for the last of the Round Table knights, they must have been good rock-climbers as well as stout fighters. The cave they are supposed to have entered is in the groove to the right of the central part of the precipice (hardly to be seen from below) and even a mountain goat would find it difficult to reach it from the crest where King Arthur's last battle was fought.

GLENDOWER'S CHIMNEY

'Glyndwr's Gully. 250 feet. First Ascent, Owain Glyndwr, circa 1400.'

This entry in the rock-climbing guidebook to Moel Hebog seems to confirm that the great Welsh leader, head of the rebellion against Henry IV of England, did the first recorded Welsh rock-climb. Here is how it happened.

Owen Glendower (to use the English form of the hero's name) was at the lowest ebb of his changing fortunes. His makeshift army was dispersed, his lands were in the possession of his enemies, and he himself was being hunted through Snowdonia by bands of King Henry's soldiers. Giving his pursuers the slip, he crossed the mountains into Nant Colwyn, and there found refuge in the house of an old friend named Rhys Goch — Red Rhys.

Hafod Garegog was the name of the house, and it stood in a lonely glen facing across the valley towards Moel Hebog, with no other dwelling near it. Before long, however, the news leaked out that a distinguished stranger was the guest of Red Rhys, and those who sought to kill or capture Owen Glendower heard it. There came a day when a servant of Rhys Goch dashed up to Hafod Garegog to report that a large party of soldiers in light armour and carrying swords was approaching the house. Rhys and Owen swiftly dressed themselves in servants' clothing and made for the open mountainsides, Rhys heading for Nantmor and Owen running towards Aberglaslyn and the sea. But if they had hoped to puzzle the pursuers their hope was swiftly disappointed, for Owen was recognised at once and the men-at-arms concentrated on cutting off his escape.

The Welsh rebel leader had now no chance of using the sea to win his way to freedom. He must turn for help to his native mountains. The wide semicircle of his hunters was almost within bowshot behind him as he clambered at top speed up the mountainside above the woods of Aberglaslyn. Close above frowned the line of precipices rimming the crest of Moel Hebog, the Hill of the Hawk, and Owen made for the left-hand end of these where a bald shoulder offered the only safe way over the mountain. Before he could reach it there was a hoarse, triumphant yell and he found his way barred by half-a-dozen soldiers. Desperate now, he made straight upward at the best of his failing speed, at last reaching the sloping walls of scree that buttressed the vertical crags overhead. The breathless shouts of his pursuers sounded close below him.

There was only one chance of escape now, and that an unlikely one: the vertical precipice was split by a cleft or chimney, nearly three hundred feet from top to bottom. If Owen could not get up it he was a dead man. He toiled up the scree with the hunt at his heels and launched himself at the steep rock. It gave Owen Glendower safe hold for hand and foot, but none of the pursuing soldiers would dare an ascent where one slip meant death. While their quarry climbed on up the chimney, King Henry's men scrambled off to the left to gain the crest by an easier way. And when they reached it, there was no sign of Owen, on the ridge or on the summit of Moel Hebog. Certain that he had fled downwards into Cwm Pennant on the farther side of the mountain, the soldiers hurried down and spent the rest of the day searching that valley.

They searched in vain. For Owen, after emerging at the top of his chimney, had run along the ridge to the verge of the northern precipice, Y Diffwys, and climbing down it a little way had hidden himself securely in a cave. And so the bold Welshman lived to fight another day.

THE WALK:
TO THE SCENE OF GLENDOWER'S
ESCAPE

MAP SQUARE B2
O.S. reference 585475
Easy. Allow 1½ hours. Fine
views on a clear day.

This walk starts (like the Gelert's Grave walk) from the free car park at Beddgelert, which is close to the Royal Goat Hotel. Turn right when you come out of the car park and go straight up through the open yard of the hotel — a right-of-way — passing through gaps in two walls just above it. A grassy track mounts gently beyond, quickly reaching a small bridge over the cutting once used by the little Welsh Highland Railway. Climb over the wooden stile at the other end of the bridge. As you do so, you see Moel Hebog directly above. The cliffs up which Owen Glendower escaped are those to the left of the highest point, and a 'step' in their skyline marks the top of Glendower's Chimney.

Beyond the stile, turn to the right between stone walls. The grassy track bends left in a few minutes, to go through an iron gate, cross a small bridge over a stream, and join a metalled lane. (If you turned right here you could be back at the car in 15 minutes). Turning left up the lane brings you to a pine glade. When the lane emerges from it you will see, peering down from high above, the upper part of Y Diffwys where Owen hid in a cave after his chimney climb.

Now the lane bends left round the old farmhouse of Cwm Cloch Uchaf, and 150 yards farther on up the hill it curls left and then right to get past some farm buildings. Here the peaks of the Moelwyn range come in sight ahead. In a few minutes more the lane ends at a gate with a Private notice on it; but a large signpost on the left, BEDDGELERT, shows you the way, which is straight down the rough field below the lane. As you begin the descent there is a noble view before you — the graceful peak of Moel Siabod framed between the rocky sides of Nant Gwynant, with Beddgelert's houses in the trees below.

A little way down the slope, bear right through a gap in the stone wall. There is only a faint track here, but by keeping straight down you can't go wrong. The way goes under trees and down by two narrow wall-gaps where there is a path with steps. 100 yards below the second gap there is an iron post and sign, CWM CLOCH, and close to it a small iron gate. Go through the iron gate and to the left, keeping near the wall on your left until a track bears slightly to the right. In less than 5 minutes from the post and sign you reach the wooden stepladder at the bridge. And from here it is a 5-minute downhill stroll to car park and car.

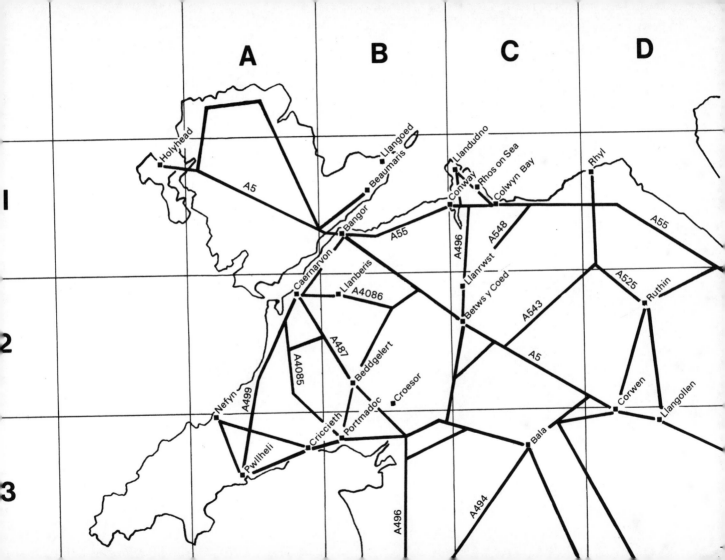